EXPLORING COUNTRIES

Venezuela

by Kari Schuetz

BELLWETHER MEDIA · MINNEAPOLIS, MN

Note to Librarians, Teachers, and Parents:

Blastoff! Readers are carefully developed by literacy experts and combine standards-based content with developmentally appropriate text.

Level 1 provides the most support through repetition of high-frequency words, light text, predictable sentence patterns, and strong visual support.

Level 2 offers early readers a bit more challenge through varied simple sentences, increased text load, and less repetition of high-frequency words.

Level 3 advances early-fluent readers toward fluency through increased text and concept load, less reliance on visuals, longer sentences, and more literary language.

Level 4 builds reading stamina by providing more text per page, increased use of punctuation, greater variation in sentence patterns, and increasingly challenging vocabulary.

Level 5 encourages children to move from "learning to read" to "reading to learn" by providing even more text, varied writing styles, and less familiar topics.

Whichever book is right for your reader, Blastoff! Readers are the perfect books to build confidence and encourage a love of reading that will last a lifetime!

This edition first published in 2012 by Bellwether Media, Inc.

No part of this publication may be reproduced in whole or in part without written permission of the publisher. For information regarding permission, write to Bellwether Media, Inc., Attention: Permissions Department, 5357 Penn Avenue South, Minneapolis, MN 55419.

Library of Congress Cataloging-in-Publication Data

Schuetz, Kari.
Venezuela / by Kari Schuetz.
   p. cm. – (Blastoff! readers: exploring countries)
Includes bibliographical references and index.
Summary: "Developed by literacy experts for students in grades three through seven, this book introduces young readers to the geography and culture of Venezuela"–Provided by publisher.
ISBN 978-1-60014-735-7 (hardcover : alk. paper)
1. Venezuela–Juvenile literature. I. Title.
F2308.5.S45 2012
987–dc23   2011039982

Printed in the United States of America, North Mankato, MN.

010112   1203

Contents

Caribbean Sea

Gulf of Venezuela

Paraguaná

★ **Caracas**

Lake Maracaibo

Venezuela

Colombia

Brazil

Did you know?

Paraguaná is Venezuela's largest peninsula, with 200 miles (322 kilometers) of coastline. Pirates and smugglers once used the peninsula as a hideout.

N
W — E
S

Atlantic Ocean

Guyana

Venezuela is a country in the northern part of South America. It has a total area that spans 352,144 square miles (912,050 square kilometers). Its northern coast meets the Caribbean Sea and the Atlantic Ocean. The capital city of Caracas is located near the center of this coast. The **Gulf** of Venezuela cuts into the land where Venezuela meets Colombia. This gulf connects to Lake Maracaibo, the largest lake in South America. Guyana touches Venezuela's eastern border, and Brazil shares Venezuela's southern border.

Did you know?
Venezuela has two major seasons. December to March is the dry season. The wet season is May through October.

Venezuela's landscape features mountains, forested highlands, and lowlands. Bolívar Peak, Venezuela's highest point, is part of the Andes Mountain range in the northwest. It reaches a height of 16,427 feet (5,007 meters). The Guiana Highlands define southern Venezuela. They are covered in forests and include breathtaking waterfalls.

The third-longest river in South America, the Orinoco River, flows across central Venezuela. The tropical plains along the river are called the Llanos. The grasslands there become wetlands when the region floods during its rainy season. The Orinoco **Delta** forms in eastern Venezuela, where the Orinoco empties into the Atlantic Ocean.

fun fact

Christopher Columbus discovered Margarita Island just north of mainland Venezuela on his third voyage to the Americas. The sea around the island was stocked with pearls, so the island became known as the Isle of Pearls.

Margarita Island

In the Guiana Highlands, Angel Falls drops from a height of 3,212 feet (979 meters). It is the world's highest waterfall and Venezuela's most popular attraction. **Tourists** travel to this secluded location by boat or seaplane and then hike to get close. They can often feel the spray of the falls from 1 mile (1.6 kilometers) away!

Angel Falls begins its plunge at the top of a **table mountain** called Auyán-Tepuí, or "Devil's Mountain." It was on this mountain in 1937 that American pilot Jimmie Angel crash-landed. He was on a trip to find gold. After people heard about Angel's eleven-day descent down the rugged mountain, they called the shimmering falls Angel Falls. This name is still used today.

Did you know?
Angel Falls is about 19 times higher than Niagara Falls, which is located on the New York-Canada border.

scarlet ibis

Venezuela's landscape offers **habitats** for a variety of animals. Seven **species** of big cats prowl through the country's forests. These include ocelots, jaguars, and margays. Ocelots and jaguars chase deer, tapirs, agoutis, and opossums on the ground. Margays prefer to leap between tree branches to snatch tree frogs and even monkeys.

Did you know?

The green anaconda, the world's largest snake, sneaks up on and coils itself around prey in Venezuela's swamps.

green anaconda

tamandua

ocelot

fun fact

A type of anteater called the tamandua lives in Venezuela's forests. This animal is known as "the stinker of the forest" because it releases a horrible smell to keep predators away!

Scarlet ibises dot the Orinoco Delta with brilliant color. Their diet of red **crustaceans** causes their pinkish red color. Other **migratory** birds, including cranes and storks, make homes in swamps along the coast. Caimans, lizards, and turtles also live in these swamps. Manatees swim in the coastal waters, and electric eels and piranhas fill the country's rivers.

More than 27 million people call Venezuela their home. Three out of every five Venezuelans have mixed backgrounds. They are called *mestizos*. About one out of every five people in Venezuela has **ancestors** from Europe. On the Caribbean coast, there are people with African roots, and some **Amerindians** still inhabit southern Venezuela. **Immigrants** from other countries, especially Colombia, also make up part of the population. Spanish is considered the country's official language. However, about 30 **native** languages are also spoken.

Speak Spanish!

English	Spanish	How to say it
hello	hola	OH-lah
good-bye	adios	ah-dee-OHS
yes	sí	SEE
no	no	NOH
please	por favor	POHR fah-VOR
thank you	gracias	GRAH-see-uhs
friend (male)	amigo	ah-MEE-goh
friend (female)	amiga	ah-MEE-gah

! fun fact

Venezuela means "Little Venice." The stilt houses and wooden boats of the native people reminded Spanish explorers of Venice, Italy.

More than nine out of every ten Venezuelans live in cities. Most have houses or rent high-rise apartments. They ride *por puestos* to get around. These vehicles are a cross between a bus and a taxi.

In the countryside, some people live on cattle ranches. Amerindians still live in traditional thatched houses. Many of these houses are built on stilts. This prevents them from being washed away by floodwaters.

Where People Live in Venezuela

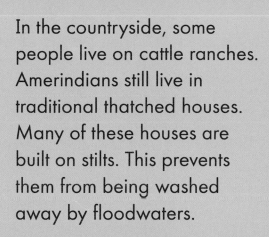

countryside
7%

cities
93%

Venezuelan children are expected to attend nine years of school, usually from ages 6 to 15. Those who complete primary school move on to two years of secondary school. They choose their area of focus. Options include science, the **humanities**, or a technical subject. After secondary school, one out of every four students chooses to continue to higher education. This ranges from **vocational schools** to universities.

Did you know?

Venezuela strongly believes in technology as a tool for learning. Elementary school students are given laptop computers to aid in their studies.

Where People Work in Venezuela

manufacturing 23%

services 64%

farming 13%

18

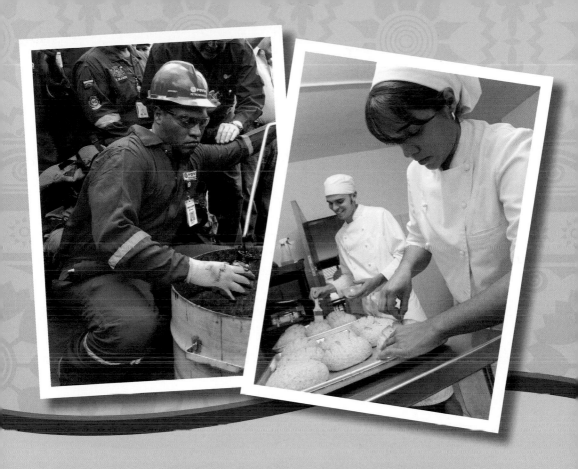

Oil is Venezuela's most important **natural resource**. Workers drill for oil in the countryside and off the coasts. It is **refined** into usable **exports**. Miners also dig up coal and iron ore from the countryside. One out of every five people in Venezuela is a miner or factory worker.

Most Venezuelan farmers grow coffee, which is the country's main **cash crop**. They also grow sugarcane, corn, rice, bananas, and cassava. Some raise cattle on ranches. Fishers bring in tuna, shrimp, snapper, and grouper. More than six out of every ten Venezuelans have **service jobs**. They work in places such as banks, hospitals, schools, and restaurants.

19

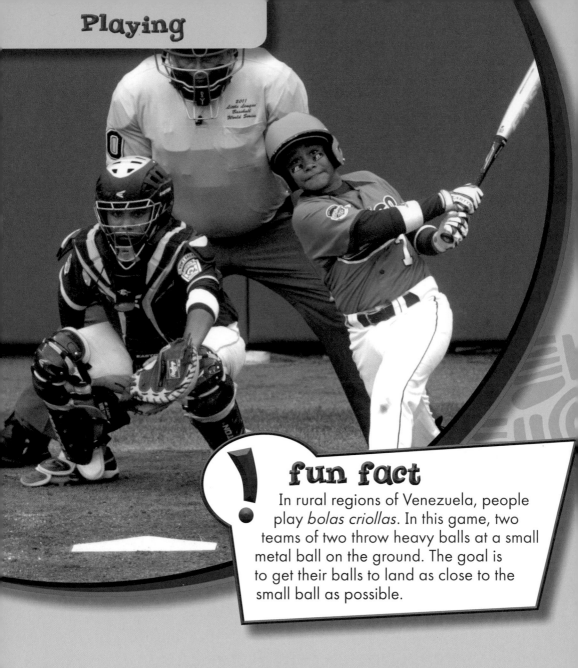

! fun fact

In rural regions of Venezuela, people play *bolas criollas*. In this game, two teams of two throw heavy balls at a small metal ball on the ground. The goal is to get their balls to land as close to the small ball as possible.

Baseball is the most popular sport in Venezuela. Every city and town has a ball field. Other favorite sports include soccer, basketball, and tennis. Adventure seekers raft and kayak on the white waters of the Orinoco River or climb mountain peaks.

Venezuela is known for *coleo,* a type of bullfighting in which a cowboy pulls a bull's tail to throw it to the ground. The country is also known for its national dance, the *joropo.* This dance features a repeated sequence of three steps. The country's Simón Bolívar Youth Orchestra is also famous around the world.

coleo

pargo

Every region of Venezuela has its own unique meals. Along the coast, people enjoy dishes that include fish and other seafood. Red snapper, or *pargo*, is very popular. Another favorite is *pulpo*, or octopus, cooked in citrus juice. Those who live in the Andes Mountains and Llanos region enjoy goat and rabbit meat. Deep fried ants are a favorite of the Amerindians.

Pabellón is a national dish of Venezuela. It consists of shredded beef, rice, and black beans on top of fried **plantains**. Another food common across the country is the *arepa*. This circular bread made of cornmeal is served as either a snack or side item. Ham with cheese is often the filling of choice for *arepas*. They are sometimes topped with *guasacaca*, a spicy salsa topping.

pabellón

hallaca

! fun fact

Hallaca is a special food served at Christmas time. Every family uses their own recipe, but a basic *hallaca* is meat covered in *arepa* dough and wrapped in banana leaves.

Most Venezuelans celebrate **Catholic** holidays. Along with Christmas and Easter, they observe Holy Wednesday and have festivals that honor particular **patron saints**. The festivals, also called *ferias*, feature bullfights, street dances, and other lively events.

Carnival, which falls in January or February, is Venezuela's biggest celebration. People watch costumed performers in elaborate parades. Independence Day is another important holiday. On this day, Venezuelans celebrate their freedom from Spanish rule. July 24 is the birthday of Simón Bolívar, the father of Venezuela. To honor Bolívar, statues of him throughout the country are covered with colorful wreaths.

Independence Day

Did you know?
More than 200 Venezuelans have come to the United States to play Major League Baseball.

fun fact

Eight teams compete in the Venezuelan Professional Baseball League. The Caracas Lions have won more championships than any other team.

In Venezuela, baseball is more than just a sport or pastime. It is a part of daily life. Young Venezuelan boys dream of playing professional baseball. Many Venezuelans have had success in the Venezuelan Professional Baseball League and Major League Baseball.

Baseball fever first spread across the country after Venezuela won the Amateur Baseball World Championship in Cuba in 1941. People started following the game for many reasons. For some, it provided an escape from life's challenges. For others, it was a way to relax and unite. Today, Venezuela's baseball stars are viewed as heroes, and the sport is a source of national pride.

Venezuela's Flag

Venezuela's flag features horizontal stripes of yellow, blue, and red. The yellow stripe stands for the natural riches of the land. The blue stripe, which represents courage and the ocean, has an arc of eight stars that represent Venezuela's provinces. The red stripe honors the lives lost in Venezuela's fight for independence from Spanish rule.

Official Name: Bolivarian Republic of Venezuela

Area: 352,144 square miles (912,050 square kilometers); Venezuela is the 33rd largest country in the world.

Capital City:	Caracas
Important Cities:	Maracaibo, Valencia, Barquisimeto, Maracay
Population:	27,635,743 (July 2011)
Official Language:	Spanish
National Holiday:	Independence Day (July 5)
Religions:	Christian (98%), Other (2%)
Major Industries:	farming, fishing, manufacturing, mining, services
Natural Resources:	oil, natural gas, iron ore, bauxite, hydropower, diamonds
Manufactured Products:	clothing, food products, machinery, construction materials, metals, automobiles
Farm Products:	coffee beans, corn, sorghum, sugarcane, rice, bananas, vegetables, beef, pork, milk, eggs, fish
Unit of Money:	bolívar fuerte; the bolívar fuerte is divided into 100 céntimos.

Glossary

Amerindians—peoples originally from North, South, and Central America

ancestors—relatives who lived long ago

cash crop—a crop that farmers grow mainly to sell rather than eat or use

Catholic—related to the Roman Catholic Church; Roman Catholics are Christian.

crustaceans—aquatic animals with skeletons on the outside of their bodies; crabs and lobsters are examples of crustaceans.

delta—the area around the mouth of a river

exports—products that are shipped from a country to other parts of the world

gulf—part of an ocean or sea that extends into land

habitats—environments in which plants or animals usually live

humanities—subjects that focus on people and culture; art, history, and literature are examples of humanities.

immigrants—people who leave one country to live in another country

migratory—known to travel from one place to another, usually with the seasons

native—originally from a specific place

natural resource—a material in the earth that is taken out and used to make products or fuel

patron saints—saints who are believed to look after a country or group of people

plantains—tropical fruits that look like bananas; plantains are often fried in Venezuela.

refined—stripped of unwanted parts; Venezuelan oil workers refine crude oil to make gasoline and other products.

service jobs—jobs that perform tasks for people or businesses

species—specific kinds of living things; members of a species share the same characteristics.

table mountain—a mountain with a flat top

tourists—people who are visiting a country

vocational schools—schools that teach specific jobs and trades

To Learn More

AT THE LIBRARY

Katz Cooper, Sharon. *Venezuela ABCs: A Book About the People and Places of Venezuela.* Minneapolis, Minn.: Picture Window Books, 2007.

National Geographic. *National Geographic World Atlas for Young Explorers.* Washington, D.C.: National Geographic Society, 2010.

Patterson, Irania Macias. *Wings and Dreams: The Legend of Angel Falls.* Charlotte, N.C.: Novello Festival Press, 2010.

ON THE WEB

Learning more about Venezuela is as easy as 1, 2, 3.

1. Go to www.factsurfer.com.

2. Enter "Venezuela" into the search box.

3. Click the "Surf" button and you will see a list of related Web sites.

With factsurfer.com, finding more information is just a click away.

Index